The Ultimate Self-Teaching Method!

Level 1 Song Book

Play Guitar

Today! Worship Songbook

Featuring 10 Contemporary Favorites!

ISBN 978-1-4584-0791-7

HAL•LEONARD® CORPORATION

7777 W. BLUEMOUND RD. P.O. BOX 13819 MILWAUKEE, WI 53213

Visit Hal Leonard Online at
www.halleonard.com

Introduction

Welcome to the *Play Guitar Today! Worship Songbook.* This book includes well-known worship favorites, and is intended for the beginning to intermediate player.

The ten songs in this book are carefully coordinated with the skills introduced in Level 1 of the *Play Guitar Today!* method. Refer to the table of contents below to see where each song fits within the method and to help you determine when you're ready to play it.

Contents

About the CD

A full-band recording of every song in this book is included on the CD, so you can hear how it sounds and play along when you're ready. Each song is preceded by two measures of "clicks" to indicate the tempo and meter.

The CD is playable on any CD player, and is also enhanced so Mac and PC users can adjust the recording to any tempo without changing the pitch! For the latest Amazing Slow Downer software and installation instructions, go to **www.halleonard.com/ASD**.

Before you begin, tune your guitar to the tuning notes on Track 1.

Song Structure

Most songs have different sections that might be recognizable by any or all of the following:

- **Introduction** (or "Intro"): This is a short section at the beginning that "introduces" the song to the listeners.

- **Verses**: One of the main sections of the song—the part that includes most of the storyline—is the *verse*. There will usually be several verses, all with the same music but each with different lyrics.

- **Chorus**: Perhaps the most memorable section of the song is the *chorus*. Again, there might be several choruses, but each chorus will often have the same lyrics and music.

- **Bridge**: This section makes a transition from one part of a song to the next. For example, you may find a bridge between the chorus and next verse.

- **Outro**: Similar to the "intro," this section brings the song to an end.

Lyrics

Lyrics to all of the great songs in this book are included. They are shown above the staff in italics as a guide to help you keep your place in the music.

Fermata 🖕

This symbol tells you to hold the note(s) longer than the normal time value. You will often see a fermata at the end of a song over the final note or chord.

Repeats & Endings

Repeat signs ‖: :‖ tell you to repeat everything in between them. If only one sign appears :‖ , repeat from the beginning of the piece.

First and Second Endings

Play the song through to the first ending, repeat back to the first repeat sign, or beginning of the song (whichever is the case). Play through the song again, but skip the first ending and play the second ending.

D.S. al Coda

When you see these words, go back and repeat from this symbol: 𝄋

Play until you see the words "To Coda," then skip to the Coda, indicated by this symbol: ⊕

Now just finish the song.

I Could Sing of Your Love Forever

Words and Music by Martin Smith

Sing to the King

Words and Music by Billy James Foote

Your Name

Words and Music by Paul Baloche and Glenn Packiam

Be Unto Your Name

Words and Music by Lynn DeShazo and Gary Sadler

Step by Step

Words and Music by David Strasser "Beaker"

Worthy Is the Lamb

Words and Music by Darlene Zschech

We Fall Down

Track 8

Words and Music by Chris Tomlin

Verse
Moderately ♩ = 76

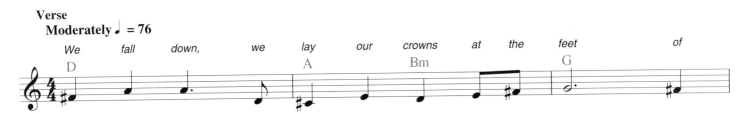

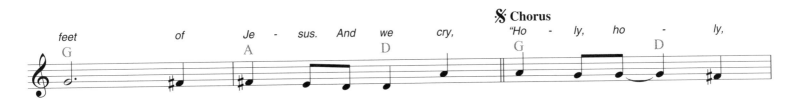

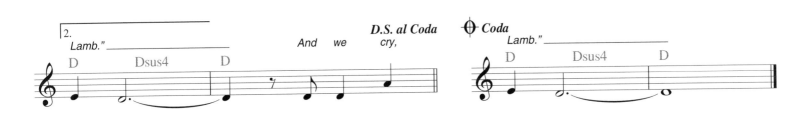

More Precious Than Silver

Words and Music by Lynn DeShazo

Lead Me to the Cross

Words and Music by Brooke Fraser

(This page is left intentionally blank to eliminate a page turn.)

You Are God Alone
(not a god)

Words and Music by Billy J. Foote and Cindy Foote

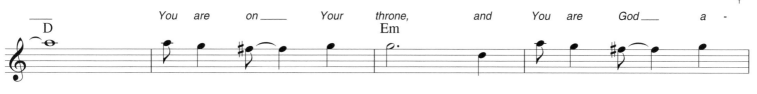

You are on ___ Your throne, and You are God ___ a-

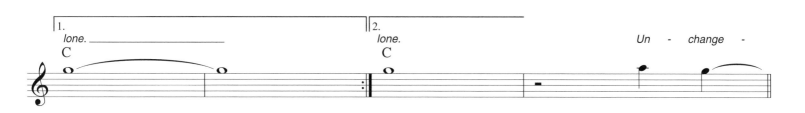

1. lone. ___
2. lone. Un - change -

Bridge

- a - ble, ___ un - shak - a - ble, ___ un - stop -

- pa - ble, ___ that's what You are. ___

Un - change - a - ble, ___ un - shak - a - ble, ___

un - stop - pa - ble, ___ that's what You are. ___

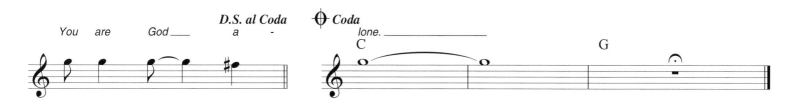

D.S. al Coda   **Coda**

You are God ___ a -   lone. ___

 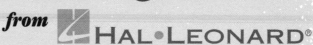